W0010181

The Naughty Grandmother

by
Judy Bradley

illustrated by Hazel Mitchell

Copyright 2012, Judy Bradley
All rights reserved.

First Edition

Published by Creative Manuscripts
230 East 45th Steet
Savannah, Georgia 31405

ISBN 978-0-615-57032-7

Printed in the United States of America

To my precious grandchildren

Banks
Houston
Dan
Bradley
Bennett

May you always remember
the laughter and love!

M000282278

**My full name is Wilbur
John Percy McGee –
The eldest of three in
The Smith family.**

I have younger sisters.
   They're eight-year-old twins.
They don't look alike, but
   They're very best friends.

We have the best Grandmother
Under the sun!

Sometimes she is *naughty,*
But always she's fun!

Her eyes seem to twinkle,
Her laugh is contagious,
And some things she does
Are entirely outrageous!

Her name is Lucinda
   Amelia Sophrana.
(That name doesn't fit her,
   So, we call her "Nana.")

Our last name is "Smith,"
Which sounds dreadfully plain,
So my sisters and I all
Have *four stuffy names!*

Millicent Mary
   Patricia McNatt is
A little bit pudgy,
   But not really fat.

Her blond hair is curly.
   Her cheeks are quite rosy.
But most of the time she
   Is *stubborn* and *nosy*.

Lillian Rosemary
Helen McGregor
Takes ballet and tap and
She'll dance,
If you *beg* her.

She'd rather read books
Than play Tag or Red Rover.
She sometimes ignores us
When *her* friends come over.

When Nana is naughty

And feeling quite *silly*,

She just calls us ...

Willie ... and Millie ... and Lillie!

When Nana and Millie went
Crabbing last week -
Way down the wide river
And back in the creek -

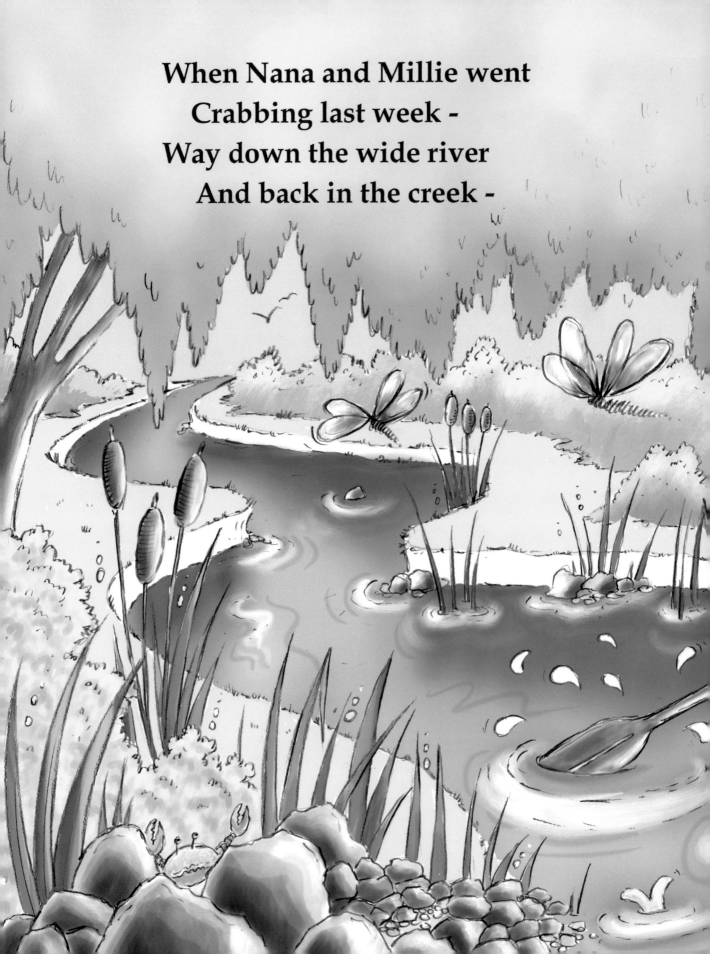

Right out of the bucket,
    The crabs started wiggling!!!!
Our Millie was jumping...
    And Nana was *giggling!*

Away from the creatures
She started to dash,
And into the water
Went Millie! ...

KerSplash!!!

Last Saturday night,
As I slept like a log,

My sleeping bag crinkled,
And out jumped a frog!

But, don't tell a soul,
  'Cause I did something *worse*...

I put that frog right back
  In Nana's red purse.

A hot day in August
(No sign of a breeze),
The thermostat zipped to
One Hundred Degrees!!

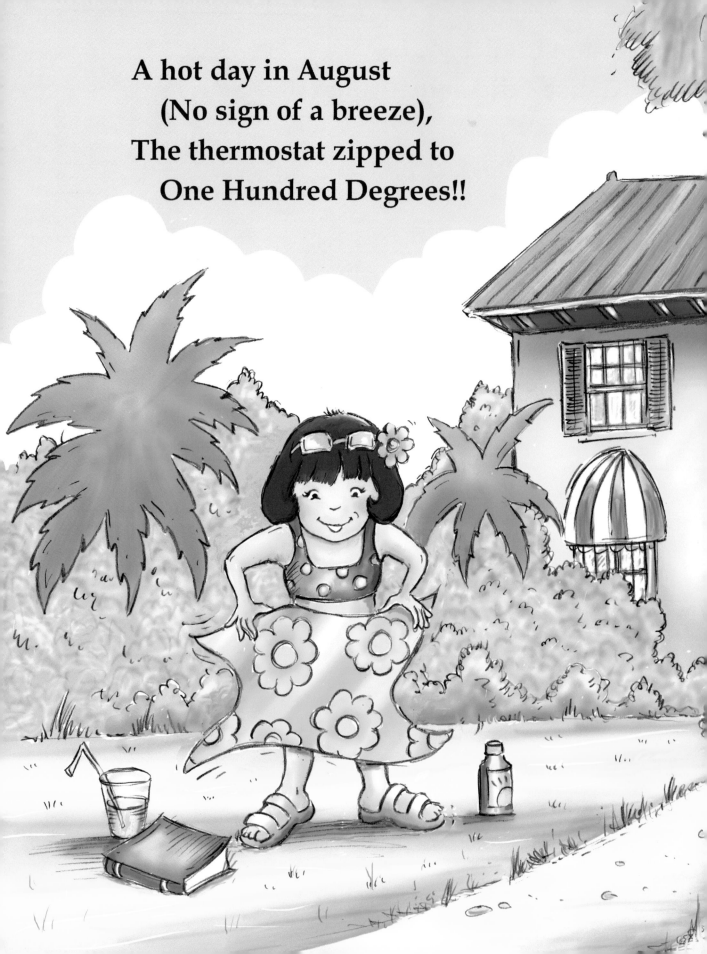

When Lillie went outside
    To bathe in the sun,
Our Nana decided
    That she'd have some fun!

She hooked up the hose, and
She sprayed it! ... Right then,

Our poor sister Lillie
Was soaked to the skin!

One day I decided to
    Make chocolate puddin'.
I added the cocoa,
    When all of a sudden ...

My plans for a pudding
    Became a disaster,

'Cause Nana had turned up
The mixer to **"FASTER!"**

The batter was splashing!
My poor head was reeling!
That pudding was sailing
Right up to the ceiling.

'Twas Millie and Lillie
Who felt very sadly,
'Cause that chocolate pudding…?
They wanted it *badly!!*

So, Nana marched all of us
    To the Sweet Shop
For big hot fudge sundaes
    With gummies on top!

And there I saw something
  I couldn't believe –
Those left-over gummy worms?...
    Stuffed Up Her Sleeve!!!!

At Nana's, we woke up
One Saturday morning.
We sat down for breakfast,
And, then, without warning,

We heard a *DEEP VOICE* say,
"I'll bet you can't find me!"
I looked all around –
In the front, and behind me!

Then suddenly, I saw
A bearded old man
With a brown floppy hat
And a cane in his hand.

"You can't fool us, Nana,
We know it is YOU....
Why didn't you take off
Your *red high heel shoes?*"

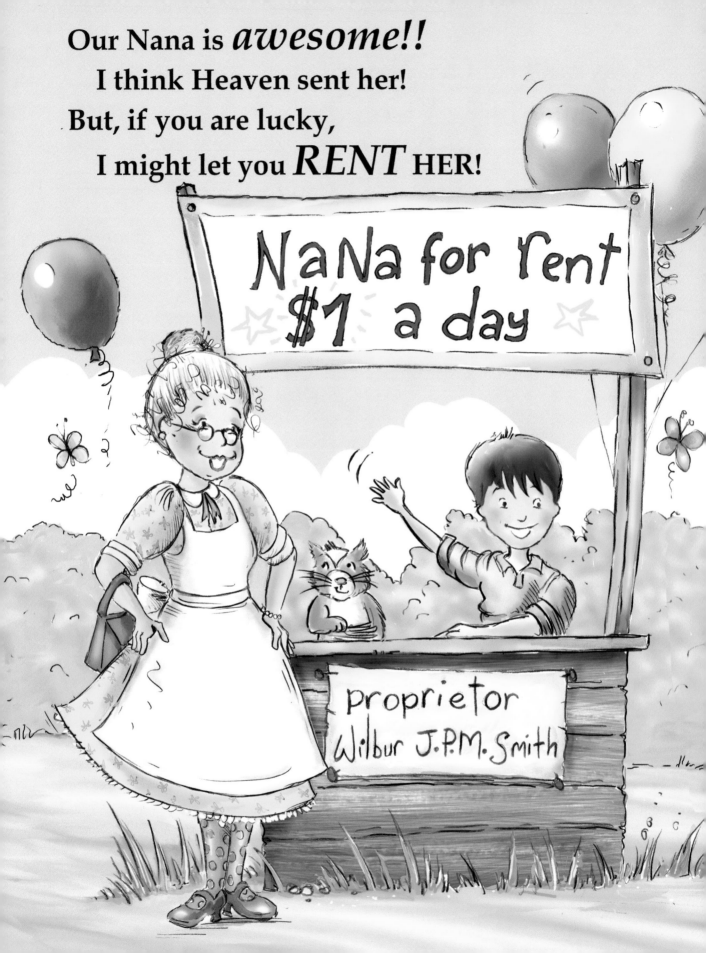

A dollar a day ...
And I'm sure you'll agree ...
It's the *most fun* you'll
Ever have ...

I guarantee!!!

About the Author

Judy Fessey Bradley is a native of Nashville, Tennessee. She graduated from The Harpeth Hall School where she developed her love for creative writing. Judy pursued her interest in writing poetry and short stories at Converse College and Vanderbilt University where she received a Bachelor of Arts in English. She lives in Savannah, Georgia, with her husband, Dan; they have two children and five grandchildren.

Having recently retired from a career in Interior Design, Judy is now following her dream of writing children's books. She is a member of the Society of Children's Book Writers and Illustrators. *The Naughty Grandmother* expresses her philosophy of the role of grandparents: let the parents teach their children the values and lessons of life, and let the grandparents add a dose of frivolity, fun, mystery and spontaneous laughter. She has dedicated this book to the five grandchildren she dearly loves.

CPSIA information can be obtained
at www.ICGtesting.com
Printed in the USA
LVIC011354050113
314532LV00004BA

9780615570327